BY THE CREATOR OF "SHEEP DROPPINGS"

SHEEP TICKS

by Barry Knowles

Dalesman Books – 1986

The Dalesman Publishing Company Ltd.
Clapham, via Lancaster, LA2 8EB.

First published 1986
© Barry Knowles 1986

ISBN: 0 85206 876 X

For Pam and Pete Jacob with love and thanks

Printed by Wensleydale Press, Hawes, North Yorkshire.

SHEEP TICKS

"Are you going to give us any more sheep droppings?"

"That could have been better phrased."

"Several idiots bought a copy of your last volume of scrawls, so you might as well do another one."

"Can I call it 'Sheep Ticks'?"

"On no account."

"Fancy a large brandy?"

"Cheers! Call it what you want."

So here we go again with more musings by the ramshackle ruminants. I hope they raise a giggle or two – they were great fun to draw.

Barry Knowles

SHEEP TICKS

SHEEP TICKS

"I'd like to register seven incompatibles, four irretrievable breakdowns, a mental cruelty and two non-consummations ..."

SHEEP TICKS

"Acid Raindrops Keep Falling On My Head ..."

SHEEP TICKS

"They're poor little tourists who've lost their way
– Haa! Haa! Haa!

SHEEP TICKS

"Behold! The Sheep of Araby ..."

SHEEP TICKS

SHEEP TICKS

"Whoever buys our lambs' liver won't have to bother about marinating ..."

SHEEP TICKS

"It's quite touching how those Arabs gaze so
lovingly at our eyeballs ..."

SHEEP TICKS

"I wish you'd say 'hurry up' and not 'chop chop' ..."

SHEEP TICKS

SHEEP TICKS

"She's certainly old for her age – what one might call lamb dressed as mutton ..."

SHEEP TICKS

SHEEP TICKS

*"What would you like to be when you grow up —
hand or machine knitted?"*

SHEEP TICKS

SHEEP TICKS

"Not a word to the missus — but those are my bits on the side ..."

SHEEP TICKS

*"Whenever I can't sleep I try counting day trippers
jumping over a precipice ..."*

SHEEP TICKS

SHEEP TICKS

"Personally I find them more attractive with their clothes on ..."

SHEEP TICKS

"I shall be mighty relieved when this heatwave's over ..."

SHEEP TICKS

"I'm exactly three bags full ..."

SHEEP TICKS

*"Oi! Don't you dare follow Mary
wherever she happens to go ..."*

SHEEP TICKS

*"She thinks that if she makes herself indispensable
she'll escape the knacker's yard ..."*

SHEEP TICKS

"Why not? Everybody else tries to fleece the trippers ..."

SHEEP TICKS

"Desist! Little lambs should be seen and not baa-ed ..."

SHEEP TICKS

*"To satisfy your morbid curiosity – I'm going to a
fancy dress party as a ewe-nicorn ...!"*

SHEEP TICKS

SHEEP TICKS

SHEEP TICKS

"Listen, Myrtle, back-combing does nothing for you ..."

SHEEP TICKS

*"What do you reckon – Sellafield blown a fuse,
crop spraying or a plague of locusts ...?"*

SHEEP TICKS

"Contrary to the popular nursery rhyme ...
I know exactly where to find you ..."

SHEEP TICKS

"No thanks – I couldn't eat another blade ..."

SHEEP TICKS

*"This somewhat bizarre sheeptrack is part of
the Dr Beeching Bequest ..."*

SHEEP TICKS

"I've got a sore best end of neck ..."

SHEEP TICKS

"How much ransom shall we demand?"

SHEEP TICKS

SHEEP TICKS

"What a twit! Fancy having a kip in a field where they were burning the bracken ...!"

SHEEP TICKS

SHEEP TICKS

*"Sometimes I think we must be the only creatures on
God's earth who haven't been interviewed
by Terry Wogan ...!"*

SHEEP TICKS

*"And that's some of my first wool at the top of Everest,
in Chris Bonington's socks ..."*

SHEEP TICKS

"That's the trouble with Welsh lambs – get a few of them together and they start a blasted choir ..."

SHEEP TICKS

SHEEP TICKS

"I first went on the skids when the shepherd bottle fed with a hip flask ..."

SHEEP TICKS

"I keep telling you, Elsie – this place doesn't provide room service ..."

SHEEP TICKS

"Oh Gawd – I hate these Ewe Libbers ..."

SHEEP TICKS

*"It's Sunday morning Ma – the hell with
getting up to frolic and gambol ..."*

SHEEP TICKS

"What's the matter, Tristram – don't you like curried grass?"

SHEEP TICKS

"That lamb is a headbanger – she's now building a model of an abattoir ..."

SHEEP TICKS

*"Let's get among those little beauties now and we'll
start on the next field-full after lunch ..."*

SHEEP TICKS

"Stone me! She must have big trouble with sheep ticks ..."

SHEEP TICKS

"I still contend that six months in choky is a somewhat excessive sentence for worrying a sheepdog ..."

SHEEP TICKS

"Double Tup!"

SHEEP TICKS

"You watch out for the fuzz and I'll nip in and grab our Sunday lunch ..."

SHEEP TICKS

"You two – cut out that filthy language ..."

SHEEP TICKS

*"He's such a keen gardener we ought to start singing
'While Shepherds watch their Phlox by Night' ..."*

SHEEP TICKS

"Quick – give me a tin of ram repellant ..."

SHEEP TICKS

"I got the idea from a kids' TV programme –
I'm calling them Sooty and Sweep ..."

SHEEP TICKS

*"I'm trying to get some kip – kindly stop
bleating about the bush ..."*

SHEEP TICKS

"How the hell did we ever get conned into this farce?"

SHEEP TICKS

"Would we like to go over for afternoon bracken –
it's not peeing down on their fell yet ...?"

SHEEP TICKS

SHEEP TICKS

"He's not best pleased about us practising welly-throwing with his only pair ..."

SHEEP TICKS

"None of my thirty-eight ewes understand me ..."

SHEEP TICKS

*"If you go first would you prefer to be deep-frozen,
on the shelf at Sainsburys or bunged into a pot noodle ...?"*

SHEEP TICKS

"At least he let me keep my muttonchop whiskers ..."

SHEEP TICKS

SHEEP TICKS

*"It took us long enough but we finally discovered
where he stored his home-brew ..."*

SHEEP TICKS

"I dread these damned apprentices ..."

SHEEP TICKS

SHEEP TICKS

"Oi! Haven't you forgotten something ...?"

SHEEP TICKS

"Those floral displays are simply scrummy ..."

SHEEP TICKS

SHEEP TICKS

"A typical cock up – the middle of summer and the sheep track's reduced to one lane ..."

SHEEP TICKS

"There are about fifty billion of us sheep, all drenched in lanolin — so how come this isn't an oil-rich country?"

SHEEP TICKS

SHEEP TICKS

"I must have been in good fettle this season
– look at my Father's Day presents ..."

SHEEP TICKS

"I wish to Gawd her old man would buy her a pony ..."

SHEEP TICKS

"Clear off girls – it's my turn to have a headache ..."

SHEEP TICKS

"She's pathetically shy about walking about starkers ..."

SHEEP TICKS

"For goodness sake woman, the word 'baa' is the same in Herdwickian as in Swaledalian ..."

SHEEP TICKS

"It cheers the old twit up to get a full house now and again ..."

SHEEP TICKS

*"So much for weather forecasts – they distinctly said
'Winds light to variable' ..."*

SHEEP TICKS

*"They do a not altogether original act round the clubs
– billed as 'The Baax Brothers' ..."*

SHEEP TICKS

SHEEP TICKS

*"I'm worried about our lad – he wants to be known as
Baa George ..."*

SHEEP TICKS

SHEEP TICKS

"She joined the Open Air University and got a B.A.A. ..."

SHEEP TICKS

*"Swipe me! That must be the hound
of the BAAskervilles ..."*

SHEEP TICKS

"We'll have one in The Woolpack, one in The Lamb and Flag but definitely avoid The Leg of Mutton ..."

SHEEP TICKS

"What a life! Last mating season – Cyril ...
this season – syringe ..."

SHEEP TICKS

SHEEP TICKS

"Stone me! She's discovered Lamb's Navy Rum ...!"

SHEEP TICKS

*"Please de-fleece me, let me go − 'cos I don't need
my wool any more ..."*

SHEEP TICKS

SHEEP TICKS

"It was so cold last night I gave birth to a frozen one ..."

SHEEP TICKS

"I'm trying to catch a blade of grass ..."

SHEEP TICKS

SHEEP TICKS

"Now that's what I call a somewhat tasteless Christmas present ..."

SHEEP TICKS

SHEEP TICKS